ESPORTS

CALL OF DUTY

KENNY ABDO

Fly!
An Imprint of Abdo Zoom
abdobooks.com

abdobooks.com

Published by Abdo Zoom, a division of ABDO, P.O. Box 398166, Minneapolis, Minnesota 55439. Copyright © 2023 by Abdo Consulting Group, Inc. International copyrights reserved in all countries. No part of this book may be reproduced in any form without written permission from the publisher. Fly!™ is a trademark and logo of Abdo Zoom.

Printed in the United States of America, North Mankato, Minnesota.
052022
092022

Photo Credits: Alamy, AP Images, Getty Images, Shutterstock,
©BagoGames p.cover / CC BY 2.0, ©Respawn Entertainment p.8/ CC BY-SA 3.0
Production Contributors: Kenny Abdo, Jennie Forsberg, Grace Hansen
Design Contributors: Candice Keimig, Neil Klinepier

Library of Congress Control Number: 2021950299

Publisher's Cataloging-in-Publication Data

Names: Abdo, Kenny, author.
Title: Call of Duty / by Kenny Abdo.
Description: Minneapolis, Minnesota : Abdo Zoom, 2023 | Series: Esports |
    Includes online resources and index.
Identifiers: ISBN 9781098228460 (lib. bdg.) | ISBN 9781644947821 (pbk.) |
    ISBN 9781098229306 (ebook) | ISBN 9781098229726 (Read-to-Me ebook)
Subjects: LCSH: Video games--Juvenile literature. | eSports (Contests)--Juvenile
    literature. | Call of Duty (Game)--Juvenile literature. | Activision (Firm)--
    Juvenile literature. | Imaginary wars and battles--Juvenile literature.
Classification: DDC 794.8--dc23

TABLE OF CONTENTS

Call of Duty 4

Backstory 8

Journey 14

Glossary 22

Online Resources 23

Index 24

CALL OF DUTY

Call of Duty (CoD) has a long history as an **iconic** game series that now hosts one of the biggest esport **leagues** in the world!

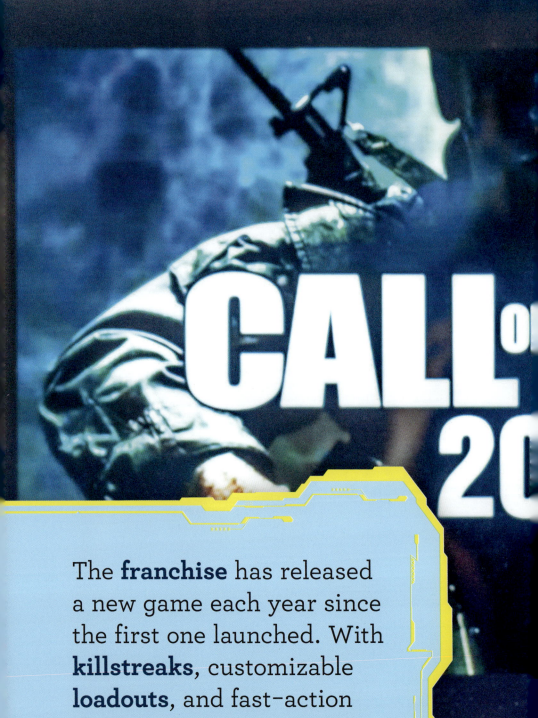

The **franchise** has released a new game each year since the first one launched. With **killstreaks**, customizable **loadouts**, and fast-action combat, *CoD* is as exciting to watch as it is to play!

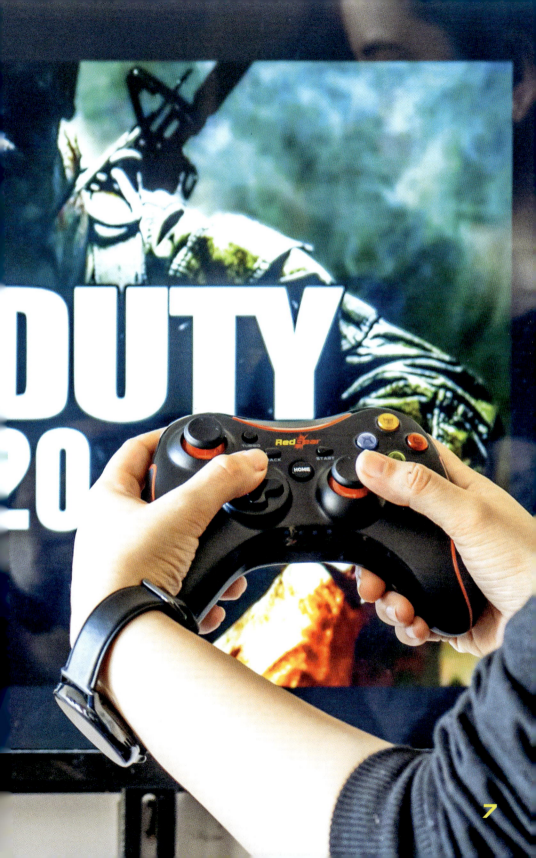

BACKSTORY

In 2002, game **developer** Infinity Ward set out to make a World War II-style game. The company wanted to create something that looked authentic and even studied strategies used in battle.

CoD was first released in 2003. It was an immediate hit, winning many Game of the Year awards!

In 2006, *CoD* became a major game in esports. Each year, new titles in the series would be released and played in **Major League Gaming (MLG)** competitions.

JOURNEY

Call of Duty 4: Modern Warfare was released in 2007. It blew gamers away! Local **tournaments** began to grow around the world. Players were able to experience their first **LAN** events!

The **MLG** National **Championship** started in 2009. It introduced **iconic** *CoD* players like Matthew "Nadeshot" Haag, Will "BigTymeR" Johnson, and Brandon "Sharp" Rodgers.

Call of Duty: Black Ops was the next game to be released. It continued to help the competitive scene grow. The first major event of the year was the **MLG** $25,000 Ladder Playoffs in 2011.

The 2011 GameStop **Championship** was another big event. Former rival teams Envy and OpTic merged into one to win the prize. OpTic's boosted up roster won the CoD XP event that same year!

Video game publisher Activision purchased **MLG** in 2016. The Call of Duty World **League** was separated into two divisions, the Pro Division and the Challenge Division.

Activision launched the Call of Duty **League** in 2020. In 2021, team Atlanta FaZe clinched the **championship** with a 5-3 win over the Toronto Ultra.

The *Call of Duty* series has come a long way. From a small single-player shooter to a global esport staple, the **franchise** has an even bigger future in its sights.

GLOSSARY

championship – a game held to find a first-place winner.

developer – a company that builds and creates software and video games.

franchise – a collection of related video games in a series.

iconic – commonly known for its excellence.

killstreak – when a player has many kills in a row without dying.

LAN – short for local area network, it connects many computers to play video games together.

league – a group of teams that compete against each other.

loadout – a collection of gear a player can collect and carry during gameplay.

Major League Gaming (MLG) – a professional esports group that holds official video game events in the United States and Canada.

tournament – a set of games or matches held to find a first-place winner.

ONLINE RESOURCES

To learn more about Call of Duty, please visit **abdobooklinks.com** or scan this QR code. These links are routinely monitored and updated to provide the most current information available.

INDEX

Activision 19, 20

Atlanta FaZe (team) 20

Call of Duty (game) 11, 13

Call of Duty 4: Modern Warfare (game) 14

Call of Duty: Black Ops (game) 16

championships 15, 16, 17, 20

Envy (team) 17

Haag, Matthew (player) 15

Infinity Ward 8

Johnson, Will (player) 15

Major League Gaming 13, 15, 16, 19

OpTic (team) 17

Rodgers, Brandon (player) 15

Toronto Ultra (team) 20